IN PRAISE OF FRAGMENTS

In Praise
of Fragments

MEENA ALEXANDER

NIGHTBOAT BOOKS
NEW YORK

Copyright © 2020 Meena Alexander

Afterward Copyright © 2020 Leah Souffrant

Printed in the United States

ISBN: 978-1-64362-012-1

Cover art: Meena Alexander

Cover design by Sharon Gong

Interior design & typesetting: adam b. bohannon

Text set in Adobe Garamond

Cataloging-in-publication data is available from the Library of Congress

Nightboat Books

New York

www.nightboat.org

CONTENTS

I.

In Search of Sarra

. . . I know that on the sudden appearance of objects that cause surprise, our intellect remains blinded in precisely the same way that eyes remain darkened on exiting from shadows into unexpected light.

SARRA COPIA SULAM

(Letter to Baldassare Bonifaccio, January 10, 1620)

Prelude

All of us live with ghosts.

This is part of what makes us human, the flesh of the invisible takes up residence in us.

This is what I know of her: Sarra Copia Sulam (1592-1641) was a Jewish poet and intellectual who lived in the Ghetto of Venice. She kept a literary salon.

She fell in love with Ansaldo Ceba, a Catholic monk. They had a passionate correspondence. They were never in the same place, the same room, never actually saw each other.

Cast out, accused of heresy, Sarra composed her magnificent Manifesto on the Immortality of the Soul, It was published in July, 1621, Venice.

In June 2016 I spent time in the Ghetto Nuovo. I imagined Sarra, our shadow traces flowing together on the stones of the courtyard. There I completed the poem 'Refuge.'

At the poem's end I see Sarra facing a young child who has fallen into the Mediterranean, a Syrian child, one of the thousands of refugees now flooding into Europe. The poem ends with a house made of wind and water and sky.

Where and what is home? How much can a body be home?

These questions haunt me.

She Reads

The beams of our house are cedar; our rafters are pine.

My beloved is to me a sachet of myrrh resting between my breasts

Until the day breaks and the shadows flee,
I will go to the mountain of myrrh and to the hill of incense.

The watchmen found me as they made their rounds in the city.
They beat me, they wounded me.
They took away my veil, those keepers of the walls!

Shall I make a house with skits?

She longed for her handkerchiefs to be revealed — lips & mouth, stretched ears to ... ill soundproof as paper was not enough ... she wanted ... to shine through the ... vague fly's away ... she wanted the girl to rise ... out of the muddy frame ... the girl who sang of the soul ... her arms & legs firey

too full with 2 Futures

to the soul caught in snow what would it like?

to the soul in a furnace filled with stone wool ... Start as I will make still

Q: what burns like paper?

A: only the soul

May 21, 2016

In Praise of Fragments

Shall I make a house with sticks?

A house of breath
For the freckled butterfly.

Will it come to me?

I grip a fistful of paper
There is ink on my fingernails

On the whorls of my palm.

What burns like paper?
Only the soul.

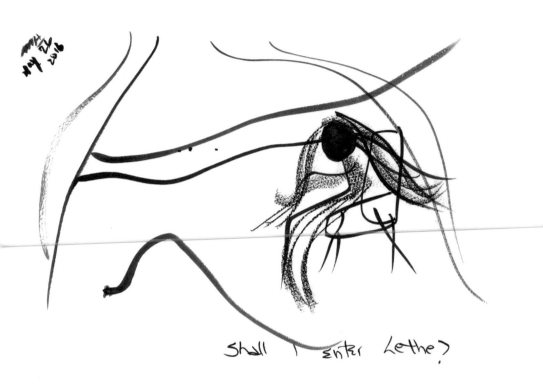

Shall I enter Lethe?

Sarra Copia
Whispers to her Lover

Ansaldo must you make music
With my skin and eyelashes,
My heart stopping hair?

Daughter of blood and ink
Thrust from a father's house,
I toss my fan into the flood

Palmyra leaf painted with swans
And puffy clouds,
Delicate ivory washed in blue.

Ruin of old bone
Blood root of language
The flickering heliotrope

With all things blind
Sucked into a dream,
Jungle of sweat and mother's milk.

A woman
In black silk
Races to the Zattere.

Remember Eurydice
Gone to hell,
Afloat in the bitterness of salt water.

Ansaldo Ceba,
Who lives by the sea
What is the price of a soul?

Transmigration

That man from Genoa—
Because of him I am knotted

And shoved into a closet of dreams.
At dusk he makes me sit

By the bedroom window
Without any clothes on

Why? Why?

Nothing I see is real
And nothing is not.

The soul sets the table
And draws me on.

No ordinary altercation
This rush of air

Ferocious, forbidden.

I tear his letters
Into intricate scraps

They sprout from the rooftops
Scaring the pigeons.

With my taffeta dress
With a candle

I set fire to this house
Smoke spills from the sky—

Let the Ganga pour
Into the Ghetto!

I'll search for Krishna
His skin is indigo

He has a garland of tamala petals
To cover my nakedness.

Who are those men
In a gondola?

Can't they see?
I am Radha now

My soul is rushing water.

A house of paper
among high mountains
using natural light
inhabited by fishermen and families

MARKY 28 2016

Sarra Copia Accused of Heresy In the Year 1621

You ask me about the soul

Look — I am caught in a net of lavender

I am drunk on jasmine

I am charred from the throat down.

Swallows flutter

Where my sonnets were burnt.

Stretch marks on the belly of the sky

Why write that?

What about the incorruptible soul?

She is the scent of wild violets

She is the humming bird caught

In a rain storm

She is brazen

As light on the beggar's face

She is a bitter crystal

That never shatters

She is light in the womb

She is the pride of angels

She is a moist palm print

She is a fragrant pubic hair

She is a drop of milk

On my right nipple.

She is all

She is none of the above

She is the star of Abraham

She is Rachel's gold

Ashes of the holy

Take me home.

Dark House on the Mountain:
Sarra Copia Writes to Me

Dear Meena,
Who I have never seen
Your sister who they say is mad
Is not so.
Neither Clozapine nor Lithium
Will calm her.
She has understood things
That pertain quite clearly
To the immortality of the soul
Conundrums of joy,
Irregularities of darkness.
She has crawled through
The thicket where the ram hid
All its hooves quivering.
She has counted the threads
Of spun silver on her own bent head
Fifty-six now and no going back
The mirror is filled with sparks.
Sometimes she sings songs
In a tongue no one understands
A splintering syntax stitched
With cries of tiny sparrows
Sensorial retribution.
She has visited me too
And we have taken walks
By the Rialto where the poor thrust

Into creaking gondolas.
We have passed rooms
Crammed with orchids
in the palaces of rich merchants.
Soon, she who has nothing
But what our love can provide
Will enter the house on the mountain—
Mazhai Malai Mary Matha
Where auroral rain falls. Nothing will bring her back.

I must go to Venice the
... on 1132
& ... for ... I will
I will take my trust into
me.

June 8 Venezia
has ...

I have played the
Violetta d'amore
what shall I buy me?

(Leandro Bisiach
dasported an imputed
dynasty of Milan
lutists)

The church which always

gives viveli in campo of manzio venes

By the Zattere

A swallow perched on a black stone
At the edge of our courtyard.
A bird of parting if there ever was one.
Who knew it could sing like that ?
Alphabets rose from damp soil,
They glimmered in the light of the cosmos
Then burst into particles,
Turquoise, ruby, jade, shadowy onyx.
Where was the ink to etch our syllables?
Bits of light tore free in the wind.
I tried to play my violetta d'amore
On rocky ground
By the rim of the Zattere,
In intemperate sunlight, trailing my skirts.
Who will remember me?

Horses afloat on
choppy water

Late Summer

It was the time of apricots and green almonds

It was the time of young mothers

Who had not yet weaned their infants

It was the time of the fig tree

In morning drizzle

And the rock dove and mourning dove

And lovers at the edge of a canal

Curled up under a striped wool blanket.

And what he whispered in my ear

Remains a secret.

At dawn, the campo emptied out

I saw it happening.

The ass bolted and no one could catch it

Clouds floated into chimneys,

The air was filled with the scent of spilt milk.

Refuge

Refuge

Under my skin
   In syllables untranslatable
With blue from the backs of snails
   Plucked from the sea
I have marked the name of God,
   On my wrists where the blood trembles
On the delicate skin of my throat
   On my eyelids shaped
Like fishes I have pricked and pierced
   With my pen.

On silk and taffeta
And muslin, on finest organza
   Slit from my wedding gown, on tulle
And fresh washed linen, on the
   Skin of cherries from my mother's kitchen
On bits of hair from my husband's beard
   I have breathed the name of God, the ineffable
Never to be overcome, the soul of our soul
   What the body longs for
Desire incarnate, what my pen wills
   Shadow tracery on this paper
I have stolen from a stack in the library.

I have saved blue speckled eggs
From a hole in the trunk of the almond tree
    That was struck by lightning
I have picked up fossils of light
    From my grandmother's grave
In my net of syllables I have
    Stitched sparks from a long lost foundry
Sieved red from a rut in the earth
    Where the butcher mounts his block.

Clinging to the fins of a dolphin
    I have swum to Lampedusa and back
Do you know that?
    I have kissed the eyes of the child
Who fell off a fishing boat
    Who barely floated, who swallowed
Sand and could not breathe.

    I have unlaced his red shoes
And set them by his side
    I have knelt by his shoes
    And watched them fill
    With the breath of the Unnamable
And foam from the breakers
    Of the Mediterranean Sea.
I want him to live with me
    In a house made of wind and water
And sky.
    Who am I?

REFUSE

April 3 2017

What I wrote in my notebook with the pale blue cover and pattern of cherry blossom on a warm summer's day in New York City, May 2016.

1.

My writing studio, Cornerstone Studios, 178 Bennett Avenue, is on the top floor of an old stone church. Through my window I see a sparrow in the elm tree. It is pecking at something I cannot see.

A bit of grain, a worm, a hole in the bark of the tree?

Its feathers are the color of her hair. Its wings are wet. It is calling me. The sky above is very blue. Not a single cloud in sight.

I hear children calling from the street. A truck rattles past.

*

I pick up my brush, dip it into the pot of sumi ink I bought from Blick Art supplies way down on 20th street.

I do not know why I am making these lines with ink and brush. It helps me flow.

The gesture of my hand marking the movements of her ghostly presence.

*

I watch her race from the Ghetto to the edge of the Zattere. Stare in. She feels so close.

The imagination in its glowing crucible creating the world we in which live and breathe and move.

2.

Sarra died just short of fifty—

I am older than her, strange things are happening in my body

Wild dance of cells I cannot see,

Mysterious empire.

I feel stitches in my belly,

Sticks and stones in my thighs.

It's time to climb the cherry tree that grows in the garden

Time to cry out to my mother

Who's gone to see her daughter

In a house by the black mountain

Where rain always falls.

Already i am in the
Earth

a thigh bone
a drop of blood

is the sun real?
who will save me

May 23 2016

this mound of mud, this
burial ground for girls
green leaves flickering

Wind Sound (A Performance Piece, New York City
in the year 2017)

Sarra, a woman in twenty-first century garb, leather jacket, black
jeans, blunt cut hair. Low, close fitting blouse. She is twenty nine
years old.

Noises from the street. There is a sound of doors breaking down, a
glass falling in the Irish pub next door to the little theater.

A whole river of women, many in pink caps with two points on them,
flood the street.

*

Sarra sits in a wooden chair placed stage right. She is stooped forward,
leaning on one elbow. One of the legs of the chair is broken. The
chair is painted black.

She strains forward as if to hear the women outside. She starts up,
paces up and down, muttering. Can she hear the noise from the
street? Her voice mingles with the cries from the street.

The lights are low. We hear her sing, a low incantation. She sings as
she paces on stage, in front of the mound of ash that has materialized
beside her.

We hear her voice.

Is this a burial ground for girls?

You cannot put me there.

She walks around, accidentally striking the chair. She stands beside the mound of ash.

What burns like paper?

Only the soul.

A whistling sound in the air. A flurry of wings, frenzied shadows of pigeons on the stage wall.

Sarra claps her hands over her ears. She hears the fetus in the mother's womb, when the skin is torn. Vagitus uterinus.

She thrusts both hands into the mound of ash. Ash covers her hands, all the way up to her wrists.

She hears the wind in the almond tree, just outside her house in the Ghetto? She murmurs the syllables she needs:

Soffio Ruah Akash

Her body stiffens. She appears to be in pain.

The names I was given flee from me.

Where did that line come from?

Words appear on the screen at the back of the stage. A matchless combination of syllables in another tongue, branching out, tree like.

Sounds of lute and harp. And a broken mouth organ. Sounds of a soprano saxophone. Grinding sound of the subway.

A boy in the ghetto, laughing. He races to pick up his red cap—the wind blows it down from the almond tree.

Noise of broken glass. Marching women sing in the street outside the theater.

*

A shadow figure emerges from backstage, dressed in a long garment of indistinct shape. Who is she ?

In the background the noises continue. Also sharp sounds of the wind striking tiles on the rooftop, the branches of trees. We listen to this other woman's words:

Ruah [in Hebrew] signifies nothing more of itself than the air, wind, and breath with which we breathe. Sarra wrote this in her Manifesto with a steel pen and ink sitting at her window above the square of the Ghetto within sight of an almond tree, its roots red with metal from an ancient foundry.

Soffio. Sarra whispers the word. It sounds in between the steps of the women in the street, the calls of small children, the ribbons floating in air, the bits of ash flying down.

Akash—breath, spirit, wind, sound, atmosphere.

In Samkhya philosophy of ancient India akash is atmosphere, one of the five constituent elements. It betokens sound—stemming from the Sanksrit root kas—to become apparent, to shine.

Sarra is a woman tattooed with bits of light. Her life stitched with sabda, sound. Rising to sruti (that which is heard, revealed)

Close to her end, she sits alone at her window. Leaves brush against the bark of the almond tree. A flurry of hair. The squirrel's nest is torn. Winter berries against indigo sky.

She and I are far from each other.

I try to imagine the happiness of trees.

Trees of my childhood, jacaranda and love apple and the sweet
scented guava with bloom clustering on the branches, coconut palm
and the giant jackfruit with its prickly skin.

Great trees in grandfather's orchard, their roots entwined.

The light is streaked with cobalt blue, no monsoon here

Sempiternal darkening.

MA   Feb/7 2017

II.

Why Venice?

Water equals time and provides beauty with its double.

JOSEPH BRODSKY

Watermark

Water Taxi

I took the water taxi from Marco Polo airport and stood staring out at the pilings in the water.

Water birds balanced their delicate weight on the wooden pilings. One bird fluttered its wings, hoisted itself into the air, then landed feet aplomb onto another piling.

On and on it went hopping and flying from one wooden post to another, tracing an intricate map of aerial flight and resting place.

I stood at the boat's edge watching the bird, not knowing if it too was trying to find a way home. The bird had the whole length of the lagoon to flit through.

But where was its home?

I had no answer to that question.

It was the season of high water.

Someone told me of a flood decades ago when people were trapped inside their houses and the streets filled with boats. Garbage bags floated next to rare musical instruments washed out of a church in Campo Santo Stefano.

Children died of water borne diseases.

There was nothing to do but wait for the waters to recede.

How was that so very different from the Kerala of my childhood?

We did not have the glories of Venice, but our rivers rose each monsoon and flooded the houses around. The dwellings of the very poor were the first to go, washed away with chickens, food grains and thousands of tiny black snails that had sought out a perch on the rocks by the river.

After the floods, the churches and temples of Kerala were filled with prayers for the sick and the ailing. In recent years illegal dredging of river sand had made the rivers sickly and the imponderables of climate change aggravated the cycles of the monsoon.

As for Venice it was said to be slowly sinking and no one knew if the plan for metal gates to be lashed to the floor of the Adriatic to control the floods, would work.

Was it foolish to come there hoping for a quiet time when I could write a few lines?

In dreams I felt that the city, ringed by water could turn into a place where things slipped out of their husks.

Where the dark interiors of rooms, surfaces of bone, shell, stone, painted canvas, ruined walls flashed with fiery kernels that escaped from shadows.

*

I had a leather backed notebook. At night I opened it up. I could hear gulls swoop and squabble at the edge of the small canal. I wrote down a few lines that came to me, then added a question:

High window to the house, half covered by a cherub.

Door on the dark side, under an old man's thigh.

Everyone is barefoot, their shoes have dropped off.

Is there a road through the sky?

These lines came next to some other lines in my notebook I had written earlier in my notebook.

A cat with a white ringed tail.

Gulls in the brilliant water.

O gatto de Venezia, your tale is still to be told.

My notebook was leather backed, with the patterns of plants and the odd animal tooled on the cover, a rabbit with ears poised, a black throated bird, a cat poised to spring, anemones, tulips, lilies of the valley, a crowded cover that pleased me.

The short lines became a way of making time flow.

The scrim of place holding the fragile present in place so the past would not overwhelm.

I thought to myself—I can dip my pen in the waters that run everywhere, stain those waters and write. I have imagined this even when my pen lay buried in my purse, its nib protected from the jostle of air travel.

*

I was Shaul's guest and spent some weeks in his mother's elegant apartment. She was traveling in Croatia and I slept in her psychoanalytic studio, a high room hung with Turkish carpets, fine etchings and set with polished tables of walnut and mahogany. Her orange upholstered couch served as my bed.

Early one morning, woken by clanging church bells, I saw a shadow on the balcony across the way. The balcony hung over the courtyard.

A simple shadow of a hand. That was all.

But through some trick of sunlight it grew to giant size, filling up the whole of the wall, twelve feet or so.

Then it subsided, and an insubstantial head came into view.

I could figure out that it was the shadow of a woman leaning over the balcony tugging at a pulley that held the clothes line in place. I heard a voice saying something quickly in the Venetian dialect, no body to attach the words to, then the jarring creak of the pulley, a bed sheet, also turned into shadow, flapping.

Inside the room, with sunlight streaming in, my own hand resting at the edge of an open book sprouted a shadow.

On the balcony outside, the woman's head, nose and lips blossomed and I saw a second head, as insubstantial as the first, turned in silhouette, pointing westwards towards basilica of San Marco and the lagoon water.

I was not ready for this shadow play.

I bathed quickly in the quaint hip tub set in the bathroom by the office, and forgoing my usual cup of cappuccino, walked toward San Marco.

Sunlight stroked the cobblestones and I found myself right in front of a child with a windmill made of silver paper in his hand. He started running backward so quickly that the moving vanes of his toy made him dizzy.

Light scrawled on light forced him to screw up his eyes. Papa, Papa! He cried.

But there was no father to catch him. The child dashed into my legs and I bent down and held him up from falling. I smiled to reassure him but he ran off with a frightened look.

The impact left me slightly disoriented. Slowly, ever so slowly I approached piazza San Marco and climbed up the steps of the Museo Correr.

I wanted to see the fifteenth century map that Fra Mauro made of what he felt was the whole known world, a great *mappa mundi*.

I was waiting to see our round earth mapped, complete with whales spouting water and the mythic sea bird roc. What color were its wings? Did it eat fish?

I knew that Fra Mauro had learnt a lot by talking to sailors who had crossed the Indian Ocean. Had they filled him with stories?

Inside the museum I turned quickly to the left, but just before the high-raftered room of the Biblioteca Marciana, I stopped short, struck by a white curtain blowing.

Where was the wind coming from? I couldn't tell. I was drawn by the fabric billowing around what I thought was empty air.

So it was I found myself in a spacious alcove at the outermost edge of the building.

Behind the blown belly of finely woven cloth, I saw her, Kore, ancient Greek girl-woman with full breasts and belly, but armless, legless.

I saw her, a daughter in an ancient story, a teenager without the legs she needed to scurry up from the underworld to the world of substances and light, lacking the arms she needed to hold her mother tight, so very tight, to her.

The curtains dangled around her. The taut beauty of her stone torso was doubled, trebled, multiplied so many times in the shimmering folds of silk.

The curtain dropped, the shadows subsided. All that was left was the limp fabric.

Staring at the smooth stone I saw myself as I once was, a girl with no hands to hold tight to what she loved and what she loved turning into unsteady shadow, making her so terribly dizzy.

*

I made my way across Campo Santo Stefano to the wall of the Music Academy.

I watched her toss a black hat onto the cobblestones. From time to time someone dropped in the odd bill. She had a high pitched warbling voice which served her well. A few bars from Puccini.

I inched closer to her, at first hoping to find a chair. But then, cupped in the cone of light made by the song, I could not move.

That night I scribbled down lines for a poem. I wanted to put the singing woman into it, and the umbrellas in the café where I sat and the quality of the sunlight. This last seemed utterly impossible to catch in words, so perhaps wisely I did not even try. And then, as so often happens in poems, the images and emotion that flows through them took over and whatever elements of will had led me there, started to mist and fade as lilies might, in the light of a remembered sun.

*

In Venice a restlessness took hold of me and I could not stop walking through the twisting streets. You had joined me and we strolled together, often not knowing where we were going.

I needed you to see the canals around the house in which I had lived, 2055 San Marco, dark palazzo with boathouse beneath and, except for the height and marble stairs, almost like the houses of my Kerala childhood.

Losing my way in the sudden curving alleys, I led you to the expanse of the piazza, the stunned beauty of the lamps lit in the twilight air.

And walking there, towards the basilica of San Marco where all the world seemed to congregate, we came upon three girls. Each fine boned with long black hair. Where did they come from?

Three sisters I imagined them to be, playing hopscotch on the broad tiles of the piazza, feet and shoes soaked right through with water.

They didn't seem to mind the wet. On and on they hopped and skipped, splattering drops on passersby, even on the pigeons who wisely kept their distance.

*

Yes it was acqua alta last night, surely it was. Daniela sat up when I mentioned the water on the cobblestones.

But there was no rain.

No not rain, its water that seeps up, out of the earth.

Just like that?

It depends on the tides and then the water pushes up into the piazza.

Saltwater?

She shook her head. Salt water—garbage, not just salt water, earth water. Everything water comes to us in Venice.

We were sitting at her dining table over a meal of seppie veneziano con nero that she had prepared. As we sat sipping wine, Daniela spoke about how the young people of Venice had no jobs. They had to travel away, to Mestre and further to parts of mainland Italy, in search of work.

Somehow my mind moved to the three girls I had seen. Were they just visitors to the island?

They had been laughing with delight, careless of the water that soaked their ankles and feet. One was wearing a striped dress, red striped with white, cut on the cross, in the fashion of the sixties. The other had a black cardigan over her short white skirt. The third, the littlest, wore a denim skirt with a cotton top.

All had shoes on, dripping lagoon water.

There was a boy too, a brother perhaps, who was standing a little apart watching them. His hair was the color of my cousin Koshi's hair, straight and black and shiny.

The boy had his back to me and I could not see his face. I imagined him to be about the age of the oldest girl.

The girls might have been my two sisters and me. I was the age of the oldest child that year when we visited Italy. Our parents had taken us to Rome, we had not visited Venice. So I shut my eyes and imagined us, three sisters in our cotton frocks skipping in the water that had started to seep up through the cracks of our all too ordinary lives.

*

I sleep uneasily.

In dreams I walk through bushes to the edge of St. Stae on the Canal Grande.

I realize I am taking you to the Scuola Grande di San Rocco. I want to show you Tintoretto's binding of Isaac.

You don't want to come. You don't like Tintoretto.

I can't stand all the muscular theatricality, you say. I far prefer Giotto.

Go back, go back, you tell the gondolier who has brought you here to meet me, but mercifully the man can't understand your Italian which sounds more like French of the Québécois variety.

In frustration you grip the edge of the gondola and force yourself to stay put. I take your hand. As I hold onto your right hand I realise I am sweating all over.

Inside the cavernous church, I climb the steps to the upper hall.

I move towards the center of the room hung with canvas and silk. Strain my neck to see the painting.

I know it's on the ceiling, but where?

There are mirrors, neatly stacked on the tables. I pick one up.

Why is it so heavy? I motion to you to do likewise.

Lacking a mirror how can you see what's painted on the ceiling?

But you want no part of this. You sit in a chair in the far corner, deliberately looking away from me. You find the church oppressive.

I concentrate on balancing the mirror.

A face, darker and older than I had thought, swims up.

It makes no sense, all that flesh puffed and crinkled. The eyes are huge.

The paintings on the ceilings pool into my dark eyes.

Then I am balancing the weight of the mirror with my whole body waiting, waiting.

*

On the ornate ceiling of San Rocco it floats into sight.

They are on an island, the three figures. Abraham's red tunic pouched over his chest like a breast plate.

The child Isaac crouched like a beast on rock.

The father's wizened hand—he was seventy when Isaac was born --holds the child by the scruff of the neck.

My hands grip the mirror and turn it, so that light from the upturned lamps placed throughout the hall shines hard onto the painting.

A glow covers the father's face, flattens it out.

A storm is brewing. A storm from paradise?

Suddenly I see the knife.

I squint hard. Unable to see the knife and Abraham's face at the same time.

Cannot see one and the other.

I can see the knife and the young child.

Isaac wishes he could become a lamb, a deer, a rabbit; anything but his child self the old man is sworn to kill.

I shut my eyes.

When I open them I see the knife. I also see the hands of the angel thrusting the knife away from the naked child on the rock.

The rock is an island.

Even as the water rises, the boy is blinded by the light from the angel's wings.

He cannot open his mouth .

Can he see the angel holding back the father's knife?

In his head, it has all, already happened.

Why Venice?

Why come to Venice?

That was the question I was asked after a reading at the Mondadori Bookstore.

All sorts of thoughts fluttered through my head.

I no longer recall precisely what I said at that time, but when I came back to my apartment by San Marco, I sat up late into the night with my notebook.

And this what I wrote. Though in truth, try as I might, I cannot recall the emotions passing through my mind as I wrote.

Why Venice?

Because I think of Venice as a third place, as the mouth of the east and the lips of the west.

Because the Nile is cleft from me and the Ganga flows through golden mustard flowers I can never reach

Because centuries before I was born Marco Polo came to the Malabar coast.

Because as a child I drank water from canals and traveled in black canoes.

Because sitting on the stone steps the other day, I saw my ancestors and they had all turned into pigeons fluttering down into San Marco.

Bit by bit, the slow waters rose.

The lagoon waters rose to make a fountain filled with waves.

Those waves were filled with voices.

The next day, sitting at a computer at the University of Venice Ca' Foscori, looking out onto the brilliant Zattere, I added three more lines.

I think of myself as a woman who has no place to call her own
and the bird I heard in the mango tree in grandfather's garden sounds
again, warbling through water.

What might it mean to belong, anyway, when the streets are filled
with water?

Venice makes me ask this question.

III.

Grandmother's Garden

Snow blossoms.

Puffs of crystal cling to the branches.

Cord of dark blood, unseen umbilicus, all that tethered me there.

Going, going, gone. Someone banged the gavel down.

One by one the flowering trees cut, the house emptied of all that belonged to it.

Amma has moved far away to Chennai, what feels like another country, to live in a small modern house next door to my youngest sister.

I am back at my writing table set in an over-full apartment. Back to what I call my life, as if something so creased, so oddly colored, shadowed and stained could be called that.

Now this.

Nothing good will come of this, I think, by which I mean this writing project will be a failure in the way in which so much else I have tried to do has come to naught.

A little silence, a little patience, that is all you need, I tell myself.

I seem to hear your voice.

The music of failure, that is the title of something I might write.
A story about my grandmother, a woman I never knew.

Ever since I could speak I had two words—amma (mother) and vide (house). When I wanted to say "mother's house," referring to the Tiruvella house, I would say ammede vide.

But the word I have now is different. It has heft—old silk rubbed against the palm, scent of fresh frangipani, burnt grass. That's how it is with language you are estranged from: it flows in dreams, and from time to time you step into a pool of words utterly old and unutterably new.

Ammavide.

The Malayalam word means mother-house, ancestral house, mother's house.

House of childhood, house with red tiled roof and sandy courtyard where grandmother's mulberry tree blooms,

House with whitewashed walls and high teak ceilings, long cool front veranda, parapet and pillars.

House that holds firm when the first monsoon storms break, when the green frogs croak in the well, when dragon flies swarm in the love apple tree.

Avede, evida, vide evida, avide, vide avide.

There, where, where is the house? There, the house is there.

3.

A garden encircles the ammavide.

Grandmother's death hangs over it like a pall of smoke.

Wild grasses are burnt at dusk at the edge of the mango grove and wild nettles turn their blistered leaves into the rays of the setting sun.

At dawn in the bamboo grove, water rats crawl.

Green snakes curl under the stones at the foot of the mango tree.

Nothing remains of the children who used to play there, tossing balls made of threads of raw rubber.

Aoui, aoui, the children cried when wild nettles stung them.

They rubbed their knees and elbows and ran to the well-side to dash cold water on the hurt.

4.

Shadows of the palm leaves turn crisp black organza, the kind used to make mourning veils. Shadows become umbrellas that go whirr-whirr-whirr in the wind. Sun cuts rippling knife patterns on the sand, and on the ornamental stones under the trees.

On rainy days ladies in saris sit sipping tea on the front veranda, men with mustaches, dressed in muslin dhotis, talk politics in loud voices, children skip on the tiles of the veranda playing hopscotch, sparrows peck dirt on the parapet and by the gravel path where rainwater falls.

In between the palm trees, at the front of the house, there is a wire that comes down from a lightning rod. The lightning rod stands at the very tip of the red-tiled roof, a roof shaped like the prow of a ship.

Amma said, We have the long wire from the tip of the roof so that if lightning strikes it will go down into the ground. She didn't add, So no one will get hurt.

Why did grandmother have to die, I wanted to ask, but I bit down on my tongue. I gulped hard. A funny sound came from my throat. I felt I had swallowed a bird that couldn't fly.

5.

Amma was sixteen when her mother died. They sent a telegram to the Women's Christian College telling her to come back. There was only a servant woman with her on the long train ride south. By the time the train passed through the Palghat Pass with its blue crags, Amma was exhausted by her own prayers.

Dear Lord Jesus, let her live. Dear Lord Jesus, don't let my mother die.

She stepped in through the stone gates. Then they told her.

The gulmohar trees my grandmother had planted stood on either side of the gates. Red blossoms littered the ground, stick insects clamored in the crevices of the earth. A terrible emotion she could not name filled Amma.

I refused to set foot in the house. Why should I come into a house where my mother has died? I'll never enter this house, ever again!

When I heard this, I thought how unlikely it sounded. My own mother screaming like that. Beating her fists against Ayah's back.

Grandmother had gone away without giving anyone notice, and Amma could have stuck up for her.

Why did grandmother have to die? I finally asked this.

Amma made a face as if she had sucked on a sour love-apple. She could have said, Look, it wasn't her fault that English doctor with the name Churchwarden—imagine a doctor with a name like that—pumped her full of gold injection. Her skin turned blue. She was dead in a day.

She could have said, Your beautiful grandmother, gone like that.

She could have shoved me with the flat of her hand saying, Awful child, cruel awful child, why bring up that sorrow?

Instead she just stood there. The folds of her sari clapped shut, brown petals wilting in the heat. Her two feet in the leather chappals stuck out. The sun was fixed behind a mango branch. Smoke came out of the mango branch. There was smoke in the folds of Amma's sari.

Then the wind started blowing, and with it came great aunt Chinna, double chins cackling. She used her ivory walking stick to poke me away.

Get out of the way, child. Standing in the sun like that, you'll get all black. What do you want your mother to tell you?

I puffed out my cheeks like a puffer fish at my great aunt, but kept quiet. All I wanted was the story. I wanted to know if someone had deliberately killed my grandmother.

I wanted to know if grandmother Eli had run away and tripped on a monsoon cloud, dark as the grave and as bare.

6.

Beautiful things summon ruin.

My grandmother was dark and beautiful—the photographs attest to this. She died one month short of fifty.

There is a photo slightly torn at the edges. Grandmother stands next to a palmyra tree. She is wearing puffy leg-of-mutton sleeves, chic at the time. Her sari is folded about her waist and fans out in tiny flutes that must have taken so very long to fashion. There are pearls about her neck, with its dusky curve.

Gold around her wrists. Droplets of gold and ruby in her earlobes.

It comforts me to think that she cared little for these tokens of grace. Something else drew her on. Pale fire that death sucked out of her.

Would it be true to say that through her death our family drew close, feeding off that bleak sustenance?

We have to help your grandfather, Amma whispered to me. He is so lonely. He has lived alone for so long.

Once I saw grandmother's pearls lying unstrung, the thread broken, scattered in velvet, droplets of milk. The velvet was indigo, the color of the sky when the monsoon breaks. The droplets of milk lay against that.

I had gone with Amma to the bank vault. The manager led us into a crooked corridor and drew a curtain over the entrance. He used his key to open a long metal drawer, and Amma, out of her faded leather purse, drew out another. When the man had stepped away, Amma raised herself as high as she could go on her tiny toes and pulled out a carved wooden box in which the pearls lay.

How had this happened? It was intact when she put it in, she was sure of this. Her voice broke. I helped her sit down for a minute, the rosewood box held in her lap. She sat there utterly silent.

I myself thought the pearls looked lovelier, tossed and scattered against the velvet, though of course there was no way with the string broken that they could have adorned a delicate throat or finely turned wrist.

Lying on the dark velvet they were just what they were, shining droplets in and of themselves.

7.

She travelled hard, my grandmother Eli.

There are letters from her about seeing the Great Wall of China, buying silks in Shanghai.

There are letters about traveling in the cities in the north of India and seeing rickshaws with huge wheels and painted sides and men crying out in Urdu and Hindi, languages she tried to understand.

There are letters written from Ceylon where she describes the great rock where people prayed, the paddy fields of Kandy so like those of home.

There are letters she wrote from Madras to grandfather before they married. He had gone to Trinity College in Hartford Connecticut to study theology. Perhaps it was in that letter that she writes: "My dearest, I do not understand this life. I do not know what will become of me."

I do not know what made her write those lines. Sometimes I think that is a line I myself have composed.

Perhaps it was an excess of travel that led grandmother to conceive of a quiet garden, a garden with golden grasses, fan shaped palmyra trees, a bamboo grove where the monsoon wind whistled, a knot of sweet mango trees and close to the front veranda of the great house with is red tiled roof, clusters of laburnum and sweet scented jasmine to draw the tiny sun birds she loved.

On my shelf in New York, in an acid-free box, I have letters she wrote about the garden, the flowering trees she planted by the stone gates, the silver birch her English friend Sabrina carried in a paper bag from Ooty, those high hills native to that tree.

Then there are letters she wrote to her mother Anna who was dying in a huge house with mosaic floors, not too far away from the ever evolving garden.

The garden as flesh, as mother space, was that what it was?

But it was also a place to work. Her friends and family stared hard as she dug into the earth with a stick and bare hands, and kept company with the male gardeners she had hired. One was a man who sported a conical hat made of banana coomb.

I do not know how to translate that word into English—the hard curved out cusp of the banana plant that is sometimes moulded into hats for peasants in the field or into vessels for newborn babies. How does it work?

A woman sets the tiny baby into the coomb and the infant's limbs squirm and shine in sunlight. Oil trickles down from the woman's palm onto chest and dimpled thigh.

You loved your first massage, Amma tells me. It happened in a corner of grandmother's garden, under the shade of the passion fruit vine—which is where your ayah decided the sun wouldn't hurt you. I kept the coomb they used but now I think its all mouldered away. As she spoke she kept moving her slender brown hands in sunlight.

8.

I am in another country. On a morning of clear sunlight, I walk into a garden thousands of miles from where grandmother lived and died. I speak of the Heather Garden at the mouth of Fort Tryon Park in upper Manhattan, a stone's throw from my apartment.

I stroll on the curved path past a lilac tree with its gnarled trunk. I stoop to touch purple fuzz of heather, I try to avoid earthworms twisted at the roots. In between the stalks of heather I see tiny snails. Their shells are the color of laterite soil in the garden of my childhood, a reddish hue with shades of indigo from the minerals buried in the earth.

Close by a baby gurgles, its limbs held tight to the mother's chest in a snuggly, its tiny head bobbing. A dragon fly on iridescent wings glides by the mother and child. Overhead clouds shift and pass.

Later by stone steps that lead down to grassy knoll I see a child.

He wears clothing at least two sizes too large for him and on his feet are sneakers of a dull green color with frayed laces he has bound to his ankles. He is standing on tiptoes, rooting in the trash bin.

He picks out a half eaten sandwich and clutches it tight. Then he brings it to his lips.

I stand very still. I do not want to scare him and I watch as he runs hard, a brown streak of light, past the lilac tree, out of the park.

9.

How old was I? Six. My cousins and I were in the rose garden, playing catch-the-dragonfly. Catch a dragonfly, tie a stone to its tail and watch it fly. A small stone, not one so huge that the creature couldn't rise in the air.

I want to see it fly with a stone stuck to its tail, cousin Koshi yelled.

I shut my eyes. I couldn't bear to see a body, that slender shimmering thing knocking at the tail.

Don't shut your eyes like that, Sophie yelled.

They'll shut your eyes when you're dead. Someone else will. Aunty hid her eyes in church, she couldn't bear to see her mother dead. You look just like her, Meena. When someone dies, their child has to cover their face in church.

What did you say?

I had to be sure—sometimes Sophie made things up. Like Gandhi having four wives like a Muslim might. Or Queen Elizabeth eating raw swan. I don't know where she got these things.

No, it's not in church, said cousin Koshi pushing forward.

He had a boat in his hand the size it would be if it were made of a square of folded paper. But this was made of tin, painted green and blue, fit to slide into the lotus pond in the middle of our garden.

When the dragonfly game was over, and cousin would move onto another amusement.

Where, then? I asked.

In the grave, silly. Just before they put the body in and close the coffin, the child has to come forward and cover the face.

Which child?

The oldest child of the person who dies. Your mother was the only child, so she had to do it.

I started trembling. I could feel the tremble start in my hand. I bent over and picked up a stone. Cousin looked surprised.

I'm trying to hit a dragonfly, I said.

I tossed the stone up into the air right under the branch of the white blossoming incense tree where a horde of dragonflies buzzed away, scratching the clear air with their wings.

The stone, the size of my fingernail, surprised one dragonfly. It had green-blue wings and it scuttled off into the sunlight, the transparent air.

They buried grandmother deep in the soil. Amma covered grandmother's face with a piece of muslin.

So the soul, looking back at the body, already starting to putrefy, wouldn't take umbrage and fly away and leave the body knocking at its tail, drawing it down into purgatory.

For Dante, purgatory was a mountain filled with fire. Virgil, his guide, explains that the poet will suffer deeply, but he will not die.

You will not die, not even the hem of your robe will be burnt when you enter into that fire, he tells Dante.

Just as . . .

the sun shed its first rays, and Ebro lay

beneath high Libra, and the ninth hour's rays

were scorching Ganges' waves; so here, the sun

stood at the point of day's departure when

God's angel—happy—showed himself to us.

What does the angel say? He says the poet can't move on unless the fire stings him. He will suffer, but he will not die. He adds: When you enter the flames, keep your ears open. Don't be deaf to song.

Close to when I first arrived in Manhattan I thought I felt the sting of fire. You and I were walking down a canyon of buildings, not too far from the pier.

You gripped my arm and drew me to the side. Look!

I stared down 34th street, a thin rivulet between blackened walls. I saw a ball of fire. It was spinning on an unseen axle. A reddish light poured out of the Hudson and bathed our bodies.

Once in how many years, I don't know, this happens, the setting sun aligns itself to the city streets. So it was that we saw the great orb about to vanish into darkness that filled other side of New Jersey, the other side of where we were.

My feet and legs were on fire. What would become of me if I kept walking the streets of this city?

Behind me I heard a tight knot of people on the sidewalk, squabbling. They sounded like parrots from grandmother's garden. It's three card monte you said. I tried to make sense of your explanation.

A woman dressed in a spotted garment was holding up a card in her hand.

It's mine, its mine, it's mine, she cried. Her hand was bathed in a reddish glow and on the card a landscape split in half by a fierce streak of lightning.

12.

Squabbling songs, that's what they made; the wild parrots clustered in the mango trees, and we could see them from the veranda. They made such a ruckus that I had to put on the gramophone very loudly to shut out their cries.

The gramophone was on loan from Cousin Koshi. I was allowed to keep it for a few weeks while Koshi was away in riding camp. He was learning to ride horses in the hills so he could become one of the leaders of the new nation. Uncle Itty told me this.

The riding requirement for the Indian Administrative Service has been abolished, Appa argued. But Uncle Itty didn't believe him. He felt that knowing how to ride would help matters. It certainly had in the British days.

When it worked, the music from the gramophone played loud and clear.

Blu, blu

I love you

Cousin Koshi crooned as he danced. The gramophone sat in the shade cast by a bamboo screen of a pale green color, tiny slats of bamboo that kept the bright sunlight out. The gramophone had a horn attached to it, and sounds came deep throated from the innards of the machine.

Cousin Koshi got the record from a relative, Auntieamachi, a lady doctor in Ceylon who shipped him the latest hits she found on the black market. They arrived wrapped in layers of white cloth Auntieamachi had cut with her surgical scissors. Black discs filled with music I was too scared to touch in case I scratched them. Sometimes the needle on the bone arm of the machine rattled and spun and a gargling noise came out of the horn. It sounded like a lorry coughing too close. Or Uncle's horse having a bad night in its stable.

When music swarmed out pure gold, Cousin Koshi and I danced, twirling our hips on the veranda, and all the servants rushed out to look at us. But when I tried to put on the gramophone without help, the needle slipped out of the right groove, and made an ugh-ugh sound, the turntable started creaking, and all the fixing I tried to do with the loose leg of the rosewood table didn't help.

Peering under the table, I could see the initials E K gleaming in the moist dark. They were cut in there, Amma told me, so that if the British came to arrest grandfather for his nationalist work, at least the furniture marked with grandmother's name, would remain in the house. It would not belong to him, but rather to her.

I ran my fingers over the incised letters, then stood up, dusted off my skirts and looked around. The gramophone was my main concern. Often there would be someone to help me with the gramophone but this afternoon, the grownups were engaged in sipping tea and picking up the sweetmeats made of crushed almonds and honey, popping them into their mouths.

No one noticed me. Cousin Koshi was out of earshot on the other side of the incense tree practicing the jumping jacks he would have to do in riding camp in the hills.

Suddenly grandfather walked in, clapping his hands. The parrots rose in a flock shaking the arms of the tree. The conversation swirled around him. Uncle asked grandfather's opinion about the new local elections and the plans to develop the tourism industry in the outlying islands. Aunt Omana showed off her new string of pearls. Do you like it? she whispered.

Amma was bent over her embroidery, pretending not to listen, and Appa was shuffling his sandals around with his toes. I knew that Appa was just waiting to stroll out into the jamun trees to smoke one of his Camel cigarettes. He would never dare do that in grandfather's presence.

Something tugged inside of me like a kite on a string blown from a rooftop, struggling to be free. I was waiting for grandfather; he was the only one I could trust would notice me. Perhaps he would help me with the gramophone. But grandfather had other things on his mind. Unlike my other grandfather, who chewed endless rounds of tobacco and played kabbadi well into his old age, my mother's father was a lover of paper and books.

13

Grandfather pulled down a book from a shelf in his library. He dusted it off and one or two silver fish fell out, delicate creatures that eat the spines and pages of bound books. The brown covers gleamed, soft silk in the lining and even the glue that held the spine together was visible, crystalline in the afternoon light.

We must read *The Post Office*, he said, pointing to me. Then turned to Cousin Koshi—You too, young sir. Tagore's play will last into eternity.

I thought it was strange that grandfather would say something like that, particularly because the copy of the play he was holding had belonged to my grandmother who bought it in 1914, the year it was translated into English. How could he speak of a book she owned living on, when she was dead and buried? In those days I thought of eternity as a tablet, molten, covered in gold, immeasurably heavy.

Grandfather stood on the veranda. The wind puffed out his white dhoti, turning it into a sail. Aunt Omana stopped fidgeting with the silver jug filled with milk the maid had just brought in for tea.

I want to see everything, everything there is to see. Those faraway hills, for instance, that I can see from my window: I would love to cross over them!

There was something in his voice that made me think that grandfather knew his traveling days were behind him.

Come on child, he said to Cousin Koshi. I want you to read out Amal's lines. It's a boy's part. Go on, son, go on. They're lines by our Nobel Laureate, son. This was Uncle butting in. Don't you want to say that part?

In reply, cousin knocked over a wicker chair and turned it into a horse, leapt over it and over the parapet into wild grass. Hey, he yelled at me, let's go catch butterflies. I shook my head. I couldn't let grandfather down. So it was that I followed him to the library, and sat close to him as he read all the parts except two in the play about a child's death.

I had to be Amal, the boy who falls asleep, still waiting for a letter from the king, and I had to be Sudha, the girl who comes with flowers in her hand, to keep him company.

It was a sad play, and I hated being alone with grandfather and having to read both those parts. It struck me that I was just like the girl with two heads. I had seen her in the circus by the riverbank, a poor grotesque thing, never knowing which way to look.

Outside the window Cousin leapt through the tapioca bushes, mewing like a wild cat. He belted out lines from the latest film song, giving little whoop-whoops in between.

Cries of parrots hung in the air. Cousin had his face pressed to the bars of the library window listening hard, then all of a sudden he leapt away. The mango tree outside the library window shook like a banshee.

Grandfather didn't notice. He read out lines in his booming voice, as if he were doing the liturgy in church. Lines about an island filled with parrots who live in hills the color of green feathers. He set his hand on my shoulder. I could feel the heat in his bones pressing down on me. When you grow up you'll travel far away. You'll come back and go away. Over and over you'll go and come. That will be your life. Grandfather's voice fell.

Somewhere in the ocean there is an island filled with talking birds. You must write down their stories.

Then it was as if he were repeating words he had heard someone use, words that did not belong to him: The isle is filled with shadows.

Isle? Island, silly, Cousin Koshi yelled through the window, and I saw his head bob upside down from the tree. Come here! I cried, but if he heard me, my cousin gave no sign; he vanished in a quivering bowl of leaves.

Words flew out of my mouth, and I have no idea why: Where is she, where is my grandmother?

When I looked at grandfather's face it was as if he had swallowed bitter gourd with chili and didn't have enough water to wash it off his tongue. He turned and looked at me with a strange light in his eyes.

I was utterly quiet—I wanted to curl up in darkness, just like the chrysalis of a cabbage butterfly. I saw grandfather grip the window frame. It took a long time for the quiver in his fingers and face to subside. Then he started to breathe deeply, rhythmically, as if he were in a yogic asana, and slowly, ever so slowly, using all the strength in his arms, he lowered himself down into his chair.

Come here. Come here, he whispered.

I went close to him and, with my outstretched hand, I touched his white head. Under my hand I could feel his scalp trembling.

14.

In *The Post Office*, the boy Amal lies in his bed, waiting for a letter from the king. He sees shadows cross his wall, the shadow of a cloud, then the shadow of a parrot that flies out of the banyan tree. Then the shadow of the flower girl.

Sudha leaves but returns. She has flowers in her hand. Blue flowers, the kind that grow by the wellside. Amal is dying, though she doesn't know this. His bed is at the edge of a dark doorway.

She says to the old physician, Can you say something to him, whisper it in his ear? The old man nods.

Tell him Sudha says I will never forget you.

15

I wonder if you know this.

Tagore's play, *Dak Ghar—The Post Office*—had a powerful afterlife.

It was performed in war time London. It was broadcast on French radio the night before Paris fell to the Nazis. It was performed on July 18, 1942 in the Warsaw Ghetto, in an orphanage run by Janusz Korczak.

Three weeks later, together with the children of the orphanage, he was taken to a death camp . . .

After the performance Korczak said he had chosen the play because it tells us something we need to learn. "We must all learn to face the angel of death."

And he had this to say of his young troupe: "The play is more than a text, it is a mood, it conveys more than emotions, it is an experience... and the actors are more than actors, they are children."

16.

One December in Upper Manhattan, with winter light pouring in through the window, on the shelf where grandmother's letters are stored, I find a poem. I wrote it in ballpoint pen in a cheap lined notebook. When I wrote it, I'm not sure. Normally I like to write with a fountain pen, but this was another texture entirely. Gluey. Shiny in an unattractive way. I imagined I was forced to use the ballpoint pen because ink from a fountain pen would have run on cheap paper. These are the lines I made:

In the Indian Ocean is an island with talking birds

And grasses made of beaten gold.

Floating seeds turn into pearls.

Things that are not, become shadows.

One shadow with two heads = the living can never rest.

17.

Sometimes I feel I am a shadow with two heads. One head in Manhattan, the other in a childhood place that exists inside me.

Grandmother's garden is gone, and where an orchard blossomed they are building a ten storey apartment building.

It's the tale of the new India. The builder drives around our small town in a white BMW. Twenty years ago all we had were the stolid Ambassador cars and, of course, buses and bullock carts.

Now all manner of exotic plumage where cars are concerned. Soon, if I am not mistaken, they will have a Louis Vuitton store in town— only a matter of time.

I am older than grandmother was when she died. I think of the child trying to draw a secret veil over one part of her life. I think of the adult writing it all down. What does she know? What must she invent in order to tell the truth?

18.

In New York City, the passage of days and night crosses things out.

You enter JFK. Along with a string of others—brown people, black people, people of all tints, all ages, voices breaking with eagerness, sore voices.

Your throat hurts with all the words. You think you know the language but the words sound so different.

A few years later, in that bleak courthouse on Center Street, you put up your right hand. You are there with women from Latvia, men from Kashmir, mothers from Mesopotamia, fathers from Sri Lanka.

You swear to belong. You fear you will never fully belong. But who could have guessed how fierce it is, the longing to belong.

You become hostage to that bright bloody thing inside the migrant's soul that says, here, here, this is where you belong. Now no one can cast you out.

You hear a voice say this to you in a dream. You do not believe the voice.

You know you are on Manhattan Island, not the island of birds.

Where else could you be?

IV.

Composition

Hyderabad Notebook

I.

I used to sit in the New Mysore Café, at a cracked marble table top
A cup of foaming coffee in front of me,

Notebook open to catch a fruit fly on a smear of honey.
The café is gone, in its place is a Reebok store,

Another shop has plastic dolls with glued on hair
SIM cards, dark glasses, cell phones in tints of the rainbow.

In a high room across the road, above carts with chaat and spiced tea,
someone sitting in a chair feels he is slowly going blind.

Over and over he runs his fingers over a page
Spelling out the names of God

In exquisite script read right to left and back again
As befits divinity.

He edges to the window, trying to peer out
At the gates of the Golden Threshold.

The Nightingale of India grown heavy in her years, lived there; The
place became a hospital, then a university

Stacked with students in stained jeans and kurtas,
A man who sold beedis jostling in pale pink packets,

Another who boiled tea in a tin can
With increments of sugar—

The bitterness of black leaves a mess of tannin
Predicting nothing.

2.

Once loitering, notebook in hand,
I saw a girl with a gash on her wrist, skirt wrapped tight about her.

She was kneeling at the gates. Using a twig she drew in the dirt

What seemed to be a round rock with a cleft in it
—Etching it deep, deeper, till the stick snapped

Using the broken bit she made a tree,
Or was it a railway track, a spitting fire, a fountain.

Where she knelt, crushed stones
Endured planetary forms

The Milky Way flattened out, Pluto in darkness. Fragments of time
clung together

The privilege of self-consciousness thrust aside, letting us glimpse a
natural language

Syntax of flesh and stone and root
Anchoring us to ordinary earth.

3.

On Nampally Road where the booksellers used to be
I stand in the rush of traffic.

By ox carts crammed with sugarcane, trucks twanging horns,
Ambassadors, Mercedes-Benzs, Marutis.

I see tiny boys on bicycles
Milk cans hanging from their handle bars.

Tyres scuff the asphalt, cut free and leap,
Come to rest in jagged loops of motion by ledges of marble

Cut from the bowels of courtly houses
Drumbeats of amber in a fruit fly's eye.

From fitful calendars,
Pages marked in red ink drop into luminous air.

Together with the wings of flying things so quick to die. Epiclesis—
the breaking of bread

And the gathering-in again: The loneliness of paving stones

Returning us to a dream of love,
And what we did not know we were.

A Notebook is Not a Foreign Country

Days and months are the travelers of eternity
So are the years that pass

Basho wrote on his sleeve
As he crossed a mountain pass.

The warbling sound of the mountain.
Is this what Basho heard?

His ink was the color of iris petals.
Where is Basho now?

On the way to Dharamsala
The taxi stopped by a cluster of goats

Their coats mottled red in sunlight,
I see a child with a pitcher on her head

A scarf blows about her knees,
By a tree festooned with plastic bags

(Daily detritus) I catch the words of a girl—
Slow hours she swung in a tree

Leaves cradled her face,
Her eyes were hidden.

She needed a goddess naked and green
When her mother called—Meena,

O Meena where are you now?
The child's lips trembled.

The tree replied
Rustling leaves, rattling its moist twigs.

Alone in her bed, the child writes—
I am she who cannot be.

What can a clump of words mean?
She hides the book under her muslin cover.

I brood on Basho
Who burnt his house

And crossed a mountain pass
He entered a kingdom of ringing syllables

And did not lose his way.
A notebook is not a foreign country.

June 5—
A bird warbles in water.
In the stones

We see a laughing thrush.
Its feathers, the color of your hair.

June 6—
In the Kangra Art Museum, miniatures stud the walls—
Krishna combing Radha's hair. Kangra 18 c.

Her skirts ruffled with intricate embroidery
Her nails incarnadine

The storm of her hair, his blue hands in it,
His ochre robe blowing.

Rocks and trees a blur,
Bear witness.

June 7—
Tibet Museum, in Dharamsala—
Bloodstained scarf and shirt

Worn by a political prisoner.
I could not pluck my eyes from precious stains

Tea colored now, in sunlight.
Dalai Lama temple—on the painted verandah

A brazier perpetually burning.
Inside the temple, Green Tara of Everlasting Compassion

Under her gaze, saved from peril,
Bound in fine linen,

Heaped inside glass,
They turn in stillness, ancient liturgies.

River at Alleppey
(On Reading a Poem by Yang Wan-Li)

I. Day River

The boatman with his conical cap
Peers over the prow,
The waves are crammed
With water fowl
Beaks flecked red
(Like her eyes this morning).

He slaps the water
With a paddle—feathers fly.
Three school girls
In the boat, decked
In blouses
The color of raw eggs
Point umbrellas, start giggling.

II. Night River

Trees swirl over backwaters,
Reeds vomit fireflies.
I pick up my pen—
Moonlight flits
Over one hundred
And one acres
Of tangled water weeds.

AFTERWORD
by Leah Souffrant

Meena Alexander composed *In Praise of Fragments* in what we now know would be the final years of her life, when we often chatted about the essential relationship between embodied experience and poetics. We shared a curiosity about the way what we perceive shapes how we know and what we create. Her commitment to these questions was never more vividly expressed than in the creation of this book. Here she was seeking to make art that bodied forth, rich and messy. Yet throughout her philosophical and artistic vision, the "fragments" of lived experience have been meeting the meaning-making process they forge and reflect.

One afternoon in early 2017, Meena gingerly opened the large sketchbook of thick paper across a kitchen table and pointed to the ink strokes with fingers as if marking the pages anew with air. Could these pages be in the poems? she wondered. How could the poems make sense without the images? The necessity of reaching beyond words was urgent. We talked through the creation of *In Praise of Fragments*, dwelling on image and word. She needed the interplay of bold black lines with handwritten drafts of poems, in part because the image was so central to her conception of poetry.

In November 2018, in an interview reflecting on poetry, she observed, "The images often make all sorts of tentacles between each other, little roots that they put out, and meanings, they are like synapses, they start to irradiate the structure of the whole." At a performance of this work a year earlier, in fall 2017, at the Emily Harvey Gallery in Manhattan, the poems were recited by Meena, projected on screens, and they traveled about a loft as actors performed and dancers moved. The images multiplied in space and time, as this book itself imagines its poetry. Different voices and bodies were in the room as they are at work here on the page. In the book, voices and bodies, across time and space, even within the space of a page, "make all sorts of tentacles." In ink and in print, languages are overlayed. Now reading this volume, the air we breathe becomes the air of Sarra Copia, walking both the streets of Venice and New York. So too the waters of Italy are the rivers of India. In Meena Alexander's poetic image, the reach is that far. Across not only time, but also space, and transcending the boundaries of both in multiple lives, memories, and languages.

Meena Alexander had been devoted to these ideas and images for at least four decades. In a 1979 discussion of Wordsworth's Prelude, she had already started an investigation of the layering of experience, memory, and voice. Here we might find a trail to follow in assessing this collection—as both a composition and a collection of fragments. "The act of recovering the past and creating a true poetic self," she writes in The Poetic Self: Towards a Phenomenology of Romanticism, "comes about through the interpenetration of the two voices, the voice of the present meditating consciousness and the voice of the embodied self of time past" (74). In her poetry, the two voices of past and present multiply to include a more complex layering. And the poetic self is only part of the experience that emerges. Time links and loops across a lifetime, recursive. But time, for this poet, is also an ever changing patchwork assembled and reassembled. Memory itself is mixed up in times and places that are various, unpredictable, and shifting. It is not me-now remembering this-happened-then, but rather a mingling of voices at once immediate and ancestral, familial and literary, contemporary and transcending temporal fixity.

In her 2009 collection of essays Poetics of Dislocation, she quotes Édouard Glissant. "The power to experience the shock of elsewhere is what distinguishes the poet" (4). The poetry that emerges, however, is not only a shock but a comfort, a fleeting clarity that sustains poet and reader. In 2018, she explained, "We're all exiles in time. Even if you live in the same house, on the same plot of land, time alters what is around you. And so there is a way in which you might not be a migrant in space, but we're all built to lose and gain and endure time." A sensitivity to this relationship to displacement from space and time emerges in this collection. Sarra Copia, who died in 1641, writes a letter: "Dear Meena,/Who I have never seen" And later, in "Venice Fragments," the poet today reflects, "I think of myself as a woman who has no place to call her own and the bird I heard in the mango tree in grandfather's garden sounds again, warbling through water."

The fragments are pieces and pieced together, making connections in the work and extending beyond it. The poems reach into other books, places, and times. They are made from and lead the reader into the Bhagavad-Gita, The Bible, the letters of Sarra Copia and the letters of Meena's grandmother, Meena's own diaries and images captured in sumi ink. Narrative passages in prose lines situate us in a present —in a studio in Manhattan or a water taxi in Venice or a yard in Kerala. Many passages locate and look. The poet stands here and sees this. Looking at the often flooded streets of Venice, she asks, "How was that so very different from the Kerala of my childhood?" We are invited into a shared history of witness and loss, attention to the ravages of climate change and poverty. The writer is in a New York studio and then on an Italian piazza. She connects Venice of the present to memory, to Kerala. Conversations in the piazza lead to visions of childhood, playing, watching children, standing in a piazza in a cotton frock. The dream world and memory and immediate living in Venice are entwined. Yous multiply.

She asks, in the first poem in the collection, "Where and what is home? How much can a body be home?" Reading these words just weeks after her death from cancer at the age of 67, the questions pierce with poignance. The poem begins, "All of us live with ghosts." Meena is both haunted in these pages, and haunting.

In "What I Wrote," she begins to allude to the cancer as "strange things [...] happening in my body/Wild dance of cells I cannot see." The cancer that would take Meena Alexander's life was under the "belly," and, months later, blood clots would reach through the poet's legs. As the book is an intertwining of now and then, here and not-here, so too is it heartbreaking and heartening, nourishing as it grapples with depletion.

The displaced woman is listening and looking everywhere, reporting back to us what is heard and seen, and—often more significantly—what is remembered. After imagining Sarra Copia in a contemporary setting, but also imagining the women passing on the New York City street in the women's march of 2017, she connects these women across time and space. From Sarra Copia to Meena Alexander, "she" and "I " are brought closer with the art of the poem, an art that is infused with philosophy and spiritual exploration.

One of the singular challenges Meena and I often debated was how to write about the unsayable. These are among the questions she has returned to throughout her work. Now, writing about mysteries but not in mysterious terms, she shares the very process of making the lived experience central in shaping the thoughts, the lines, the poetry itself. She writes, "I wrote down a few lines that came to me, then added a question." The question is rather abstract: "Is there a road to the sky?" We can take this as symbolic, yet the probing sincerity of Meena's work leaves the reader sensitive to questions of mortality, including the poet's own. For Meena, a spiritual reality was always near.

She traces her thinking not only through what she sees, but through words, found in books and in letters. We explore with her the ways words written decades and even centuries ago are both intimate and holding us at distance. The intimacy of her grandmother's letters, "on my shelf in New York, in an acid-free box" brings us across time, beyond death. Now, Meena Alexander's words are the thread connecting us to her ideas, her thoughts, her experiences. Now those letters are destined for her archive in the New York Public Library.

A sensitivity to lost words haunts this book. "What burns like paper? Only the soul." These words appear in typeface and are echoed in ink, hand written alongside gestural lines of black texture. The hand of the poet moves over the paper as the mind of the poet moves across the line of verse. I hear the words of Bulgakov insisting "Manuscripts don't burn"; even the burned lines of poetry are not quite lost. Later, she insists: "Nothing I see is real/ And nothing is not."

As if speaking across time, as Sarra Copia spoke to her through her books and the echoes of Venice, she tells the reader of her writing process and her anxieties. We are drawn close to her even as time persists in broadening the gap between now—when we read this work—and then—when we sat together over a coffee in Manhattan or she sat alone in the artist's studio writing. Each image of memory is necessary and limited, and the insights Meena Alexander—as a teacher, friend, poet, thinker—gives are necessary too. The limits become less fixed as we imagine reaching across time to craft new interstices of understanding. The voice of the poet returns. Sarra Copia speaks through her writing in the 17th century to us now. Children's laughter in 1950s India reverberates. The memories might become the experience of now, for the poet and for the reader.

Together, Meena and I reflected on the ways what is unsayable not only reaches through but can dwell stubbornly silent in poetry. There are encounters here recorded in this book of poems but also projected into the future. I might have talked to her about Heidegger, whom she wrote about in her earliest scholarly work, and I think about how we might have looked at "The Origin of The Work of Art," to frame this project this way: "Projective saying is saying which, in preparing the sayable, simultaneously brings the unsayable as such into a world." The poet is both saying and putting forth what is unsayable.

Over and over, the writing insists on the soul mingling with materiality of book and body. "Can't they see?/I am Radha now//My soul is rushing water." Is this symbol of the human soul the poet, writing in Manhattan, or the Jewish theologian-heretic writing in the Venice ghetto 500 years earlier? I, you, and she become intermingled, as the rivers are the rivers of memory and forgetting and the poetic image beyond the sayable. A different kind of "shock of elsewhere" emerges, transcendent. The fragments are not something broken to be fixed but a necessary part of a larger puzzle to be understood as the pieces fit together, not two by two, but in intricate, surprising formations. The book is in praise of fragments, the poetry blurs and builds from what is, what was, what might be. These fragments link us to the past and project the poet's vision into yours, as if she writes, "Dear Reader, Whom I have never seen..." We are invited to attend to this new experience, the never seen becoming intimately connected through writing, greeting the unsayable of the soul that Meena Alexander explored with such careful attention.

FEBRUARY 2019

ACKNOWLEDGEMENTS

Some poems first appeared in the following journals:

Arkansas Review: "Transmigration"

Bennington Review: "Refuge"

Massachusetts Review: "Sarra Copia Accused of Heresy in the Year 1621"; "Dark House on the Mountain, Sarra Copia Writes to me"

Meridians: Feminism, Race, Transnationalism: "Hyderabad Notebook"

Rattle: 'A Notebook is not a Foreign Country'

"Future Perfect" first appeared in Meena Alexander's chapbook *Dreaming in Shimla: Letter to My Mother* (Shimla: Indian Institute of Advanced Study, 2015)

"Grandmother's Garden" was published in *Immigrant Voices: Twenty First Century Stories.* eds. Obejas and Bayes (Chicago: Great Books Foundation, 2014

Thank you to John Carimando who prepared all the illustrations for publication.

NOTES BY MEENA ALEXANDER

On June 16, 2016 I read the first cycle of these poems at the Palazzo Fontana, Venice, as part of the celebrations for the 500th anniversary of the Ghetto Nuovo organized by Beit Venezia: A Home for Jewish Culture. My gratitude to Helen W. Drutt for her warmth and support and for funding my travel and stay in Venice through the Maurice English Poetry Award. My thanks to Shaul Bassi who introduced me to Sarra Copia, for years of long friendship and for this visionary project celebrating 500 years of the Ghetto Nuovo.

I am indebted to Don Haran: *Sarra Copia Sulam, Jewish Poet and Intellectual in Seventeenth Century Venice —The Works of Sarra Copia Sulam in Verse and Prose, Along with Writings of her Contemporaries in her Praise, Condemnation or Defense*, edited and translated by Don Haran (Chicago: University of Chicago Press, 2009). The quotation from her 1620 letter is drawn from this text.

"She reads": Standing at her window on a cold winter's morning Sarra reads lines from the Biblical Song of Solomon I: 7; 1:13; 4:6; 5:7.

An earlier version of "Wind Sound" was performed at the James Gallery, CUNY Graduate Center by Iris Cushing and Daisy Atterbury, Sept 29, 2016.

Under the title "In Praise of Fragments" a selection of my poems were staged in New York City at the Emily Harvey Gallery, Nov 3 and 4th, 2017 under the direction of Elizabeth Coffman and with George Drance theatrical director and the actors Margi Sharp Douglas and Leslie Lewis from the Magis Theater

Warm thanks to Elizabeth Coffman, filmmaker and director for her rich understanding of Sarra's life, and for guiding me through many difficulties of interpretation; to Ghiora Aharoni for his artwork evoking strangers on this earth; to Rita Dove and Esther Schor who share my fascination with a woman gone ahead, and who have their own Sarra Copia poems.

As I was working on the final draft of these poems Leah Souffrant read the text with care and offered valuable suggestions on image and text, Wallis Wilde Menozzi offered her ear, so sensitive to sound and sense, and Anita Pinzi with her characteristic grace rendered these poems in Italian.

Section 2 of "What I wrote in my notebook with the pattern of cherry blossoms" first began as a letter to Kimiko Hahn, we were writing stanzas back and forth to each other.

David Lelyveld traveled with me to Venice and put up with the odd hours of the night when I composed these poems, he read Hebrew to me so I could feel out the sounds Sarra knew, wrote out the word Ruah, shared these days and nights in this season of flickering light and sudden flaring illumination.

MEENA ALEXANDER

MEENA ALEXANDER (1951-2018) was born in Allahabad, India. She turned five on the Indian Ocean, on the journey with her mother from India to Sudan. She was raised both in Kerala, South India and in Khartoum, Sudan. Her books of poetry include *Atmospheric Embroidery, Birthplace with Buried Stones, Quickly Changing River, Raw Silk,* and *Illiterate Heart.* Her prose writings on trauma, migration and memory collected in *The Shock of Arrival: Reflections on Postcolonial Experience* and *Poetics of Dislocation* are relevant to the evolving understanding of postcoloniality. A book of essays on her work has appeared: *Passage to Manhattan: Critical Essays on Meena Alexander* (eds. Lopamudra Basu and Cynthia Leenerts). She has also published two novels: *Nampally Road* and *Manhattan Music.* Her academic studies include *The Poetic Self: Towards a Phenomenology of Romanticism* and *Women in Romanticism: Mary Wollstonecraft, Dorothy Wordsworth and Mary Shelley.* She edited *Indian Love Poems* and wrote the critically acclaimed memoir *Fault Lines* (picked as one of *Publishers Weekly's* Best Books of the year). Alexander was the recipient of the 2009 Distinguished Achievement Award in Literature from the South Asian Literary Association (an organization allied to the Modern Languages Association) for contributions to American literature. She was Distinguished Professor of English and Women's Studies at the City University of New York and taught in the PhD Program in English at CUNY Graduate Center and in the English Department at Hunter College.

LEAH SOUFFRANT, MFA, PhD, is the author of *Plain Burned Things: A Poetics of the Unsayable.* She teaches at New York University.

NIGHTBOAT BOOKS

Nightboat Books, a nonprofit organization, seeks to develop audiences for writers whose work resists convention and transcends boundaries. We publish books rich with poignancy, intelligence, and risk. Please visit nightboat.org to learn about our titles and how you can support our future publications.

The following individuals have supported the publication of this book. We thank them for their generosity and commitment to the mission of Nightboat Books:

Kazim Ali
Anonymous
Jean C. Ballantyne
Photios Giovanis
Amanda Greenberger
Sangamithra Iyer
Anne Marie Macari
Elizabeth Madans
Elizabeth Motika
Rajini Srikanth
Benjamin Taylor
Jerrie Whitfield & Richard Motika
Ronaldo V. Wilson and Dallas W. Bauman III
Karen Tei Yamashita

In addition, this book has been made possible, in part, by grants from the National Endowment for the Arts and the New York State Council on the Arts Literature Program.

when words flee from me
the light takes over

MA
Dec 30 2016
4:30 Am

says the woman with tatoos

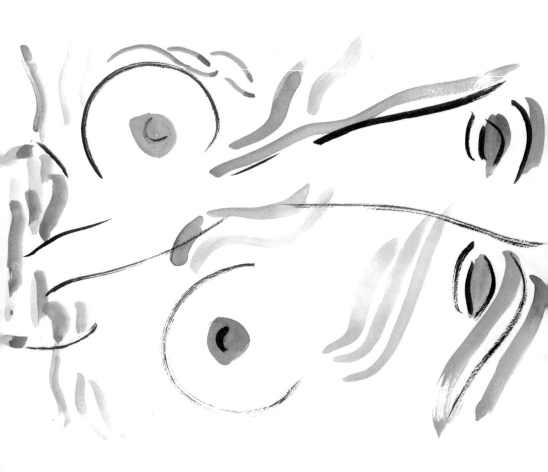